HIGHER

MODERN STUDIES
2007-2009

© Scottish Qualifications Authority

First exam published in 2007.
Published by Bright Red Publishing Ltd, 6 Stafford Street, Edinburgh EH3 7AU
tel: 0131 220 5804 fax: 0131 220 6710 info@brightredpublishing.co.uk www.brightredpublishing.co.uk

ISBN 978-1-84948-066-6

A CIP Catalogue record for this book is available from the British Library.

Bright Red Publishing is grateful to the copyright holders, as credited on the final page of the book, for permission to use their material.
Every effort has been made to trace the copyright holders and to obtain their permission for the use of copyright material.
Bright Red Publishing will be happy to receive information allowing us to rectify any error or omission in future editions.

In Paper 1, there is one 15 mark essay on each
Study Theme, as opposed to 10 mark descriptive
or analytical items.

Paper 1 is now worth 60 marks as opposed to 50
under the old examination.

There is now only one Decision Making Exercise
contained in Paper 2. Some of the Study Themes
have been re-titled to reflect changes in content.

[BLANK PAGE]

ModStds/SQP285

Modern Studies   Time: 1 hour 30 mins   NATIONAL
Higher   QUALIFICATIONS
Paper 1
Specimen Question Paper
for use in and after 2007

Candidates should answer **FOUR** questions:

ONE from Section A
and
ONE from Section B
and
ONE from Section C
and
ONE OTHER from **EITHER** Section A **OR** Section C

Each question is worth 15 marks.

Section A: Political Issues in the United Kingdom.

Section B: Social Issues in the United Kingdom.

Section C: International Issues.

SCOTTISH
QUALIFICATIONS
AUTHORITY

SECTION A—Political Issues in the United Kingdom
Each question is worth 15 marks

STUDY THEME 1A: DEVOLVED DECISION MAKING IN SCOTLAND

Question A1

To what extent are the functions of local authorities limited by the Scottish and United Kingdom Parliaments?

STUDY THEME 1B: DECISION MAKING IN CENTRAL GOVERNMENT

Question A2

Critically examine the view that pressure groups are a threat to democracy.

STUDY THEME 1C: POLITICAL PARTIES AND THEIR POLICIES (INCLUDING THE SCOTTISH DIMENSION)

Question A3

With reference to at least two political parties:

To what extent do their policies on **two** of the following differ?

           Education   Law and Order   Taxation

STUDY THEME 1D: ELECTORAL SYSTEMS, VOTING AND POLITICAL ATTITUDES

Question A4

Some factors are more important than others in influencing voting behaviour.

Discuss.

SECTION B — Social Issues in the United Kingdom
Each question is worth 15 marks

STUDY THEME 2: WEALTH AND HEALTH INEQUALITIES IN THE UNITED KINGDOM

Question B5

To what extent is there a link between income and health?

Question B6

Critically examine the success of recent government measures to reduce gender inequalities.

SECTION C — International Issues
Each question is worth 15 marks

STUDY THEME 3A: THE REPUBLIC OF SOUTH AFRICA

Question C7

To what extent do different groups live separate and unequal lives?

STUDY THEME 3B: THE PEOPLE'S REPUBLIC OF CHINA

Question C8

There is little demand for political reform because of recent gains from economic and social reform.

Discuss.

STUDY THEME 3C: THE UNITED STATES OF AMERICA

Question C9

Assess the effectiveness of government policies to reduce economic and social inequalities.

STUDY THEME 3D: THE EUROPEAN UNION

Question C10

Assess the effectiveness of the European Parliament in EU decision making.

STUDY THEME 3E: THE POLITICS OF DEVELOPMENT IN AFRICA

Question C11

With reference to specific African countries (excluding the Republic of South Africa):

Government domestic policies have been the main obstacles to economic and social development.

Discuss.

STUDY THEME 3F: GLOBAL SECURITY

Question C12

To what extent have there been changes in both the role and membership of NATO?

[END OF SPECIMEN QUESTION PAPER]

ModStds/SQP285

Modern Studies

Higher

Paper 2

Decision Making Exercise

Specimen Question Paper
for use in and after 2007

Time: 1 hour 15 mins

NATIONAL
QUALIFICATIONS

Summary of Decision Making Exercise

You are a leading academic in the field of social policy. You have been asked to prepare a report for the Scottish Executive in which you recommend or reject the proposal to introduce means testing for the provision of personal care for elderly people in Scotland.

Before beginning the task, you must answer a number of evaluating questions (Questions 1-3) based on the source material provided. The source material is:

SOURCE A: Caring for the Elderly

SOURCE B1: Say "No" to Means Testing Personal Care!

SOURCE B2: Say "Yes" to Means Testing Personal Care!

SOURCE C: Statistical Information

SCOTTISH
QUALIFICATIONS
AUTHORITY

SOURCE A: CARING FOR THE ELDERLY

Providing care for our elderly is one of the biggest challenges facing today's politicians. The percentage of elderly people in the UK population is projected to grow while that of working age will decline significantly. This has serious consequences for the Welfare State.

5   Social Security is the largest item of Government spending, followed by health care. NHS treatment is free at the point of use though with some exceptions. Apart from Child Benefit, most social security benefits are not provided universally. For most benefits the claimant has to have paid National Insurance contributions when working or undergo a "means test" to prove they are entitled to help from public funds.

10   The elderly receive a state retirement pension based on their National Insurance contributions. This pension on its own is not adequate to finance a comfortable old age. Many elderly people now have additional pensions. However, those with only the state pension can apply for means tested benefits to help with the cost of living.

Most elderly people stay in the house they grew old in. Many need personal care to
15   allow them to lead as normal a life as possible. Having assessed their needs, local authorities are responsible for organising care packages for the elderly. These packages involve personal care which includes regular visits by carers to help with washing, dressing and preparing meals. Elderly people who enter sheltered housing or a residential home also receive personal care.

20   In 2002, following the recommendations of the Sutherland Report, the Scottish Executive introduced free personal care for all elderly people in Scotland. In other parts of the UK, personal care is still means tested. Even so the majority of elderly people in England do receive free personal care with only the better off having to contribute to their care costs. Nursing care, like other forms of NHS medical care, is provided
25   without charge.

The effects of free personal care have been controversial. In Scotland, its take up rate has gone up dramatically, suggesting it is meeting a need but at a reported cost of over £150 million in 2005–2006. Critics argue that these resources are taking away from more pressing priorities and that the Scottish Executive should introduce means testing.

Newspaper Editorial

SOURCE B1:   SAY "NO" TO MEANS TESTING PERSONAL CARE!

Free personal care has been a Scottish success story. Our old people deserve it. Throughout their working lives they paid contributions into a Welfare State they believed would provide for them in their old age.

5   It is not realistic to claim that nursing and personal care can be separated. The Sutherland Report was right to say that an elderly person with dementia in a residential home should have their personal care funded in the same way as any elderly NHS hospital patient. Furthermore, the majority of elderly people do not claim those benefits which are means tested. Local authority tenants lose a smaller percentage of their income than owner occupiers even though they are more likely to claim. In
10 England, elderly people with savings have to use them to pay for personal care. Why should they be penalised for thrift? The English system is so complex that health authorities have had to review all long term care cases and pay out £500 million to elderly people who were wrongly assessed.

Free personal care is entirely within the original aims of the Welfare State. If its cost is
15 a problem then it can easily be solved. The Scottish Executive has the power to increase Income Tax in Scotland by up to 3p in the pound. It should be prepared to do this for the sake of our old folk rather than expose them to the terrible consequences of means testing!

Patricia Sweeney

SOURCE B2:   SAY "YES" TO MEANS TESTING PERSONAL CARE!

Free personal care is not in line with the original aims of the Welfare State. It is not sensible to have one benefit for the elderly paid out universally when others are subject to conditions. Irrespective of where they live in the UK, the elderly should receive identical treatment. Some people want free personal care provided throughout the UK.
5   However, this would cost £1 billion per year and use up resources that could be more usefully spent elsewhere.

Many elderly people are comfortably off and well able to pay for their personal care. Those who are less fortunate are already provided for. The elderly already get the biggest share of government spending on benefits despite the fact that a higher
15 percentage of families with children live on very low incomes.

In Scotland, free personal care is not working. The Scottish Executive does not provide local authorities with sufficient funding. There are too few places in local authority residential homes. Places in private residential homes are too expensive for many. This aggravates bed blocking in NHS hospitals at huge extra cost to the taxpayer.

20 Scottish politicians should accept they made a huge mistake when they introduced free personal care for the elderly. There is no doubt that means testing represents best value. It is time to stop spending millions of pounds on people who do not need financial help and instead target resources on those who do.

Edwin Hughes

[Turn over for Source C on *Pages four* and *five*

SOURCE C: STATISTICAL INFORMATION

SOURCE C1: Estimated % increases within the UK population

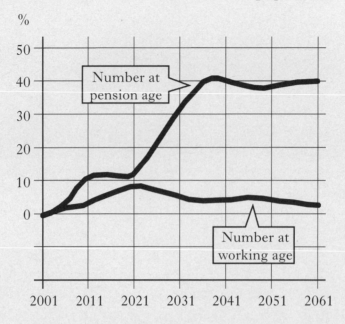

Source: House of Lords Economic Affairs Committee

SOURCE C2: Benefits and income for certain groups in the UK

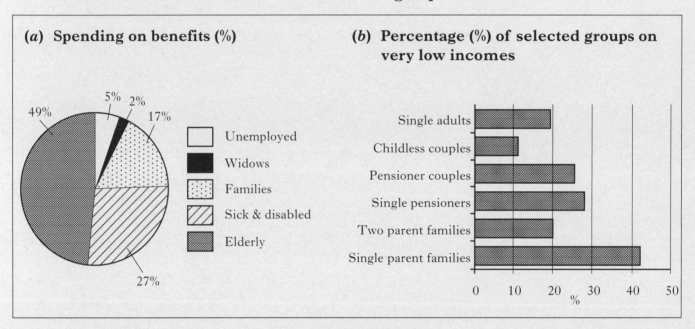

(a) **Spending on benefits (%)**

Unemployed
Widows
Families
Sick & disabled
Elderly

(b) **Percentage (%) of selected groups on very low incomes**

Adapted from Social Trends

SOURCE C3: Take up of means tested benefits by the elderly

	Claiming all their Entitlement	Claiming some Entitlement	Claiming no Entitlement	% Effects on Income*
Local Authority/ Housing Association tenant	78	15	8	−41·1
Owner occupier	45	10	45	−12·8
All pensioners	64	13	23	−25·6

* of not claiming full entitlement

Adapted from a Family Resources Survey

DECISION MAKING EXERCISE

QUESTIONS

Marks

Questions 1 to 3 are based on Sources A to C on pages 2–4.   Answer Questions 1 to 3 before attempting Question 4.

In Questions 1 to 3, use only the Sources described in each question.

Question 1   *Use* **only** *Source C1 and Source A.*

Give evidence for and against the view in the newspaper editorial.

2

Question 2   *Use* **only** *Source C2(a), Source C2(b) and Source B2.*

To what extent has Edwin Hughes been selective in the use of facts?

4

Question 3   *Use* **only** *Source C3 and Source B1.*

To what extent does the evidence support Patricia Sweeney?

4

(10)

Page one (Insert)

Marks

Question 4

DECISION MAKING TASK

You are a leading academic in the field of social policy. You have been asked to prepare a report for the Scottish Executive in which you recommend or reject the proposal to introduce means testing for the provision of personal care for elderly people in Scotland.

Your answer should be written in a style appropriate to a *report*.

Your report should:

- recommend or reject the proposal to means test personal care for elderly people in Scotland

- provide arguments to support your decision

- identify and comment on any arguments which may be presented by those who oppose your decision

- refer to all the Sources provided

  AND

- <u>must</u> include relevant background knowledge.

The written and statistical sources which have been provided are:

SOURCE A: Caring for the Elderly

SOURCE B1:   Say "No" to Means Testing Personal Care!

SOURCE B2:   Say "Yes" to Means Testing Personal Care!

SOURCE C: Statistical Information

(20)

Total: 30 Marks

[END OF SPECIMEN QUESTION PAPER]

[BLANK PAGE]

X236/301

NATIONAL QUALIFICATIONS 2007

TUESDAY, 22 MAY 9.00 AM – 10.30 AM

MODERN STUDIES
HIGHER
Paper 1

Candidates should answer **FOUR** questions:

*   **ONE** from Section A

and

*   **ONE** from Section B

and

*   **ONE** from Section C

and

*   **ONE OTHER** from <u>**EITHER**</u> Section A <u>**OR**</u> Section C

Section A: Political Issues in the United Kingdom.

Section B: Social Issues in the United Kingdom.

Section C: International Issues.

Each question is worth 15 marks.

SCOTTISH
QUALIFICATIONS
AUTHORITY
©

SECTION A—Political Issues in the United Kingdom
Each question is worth 15 marks

STUDY THEME 1A: DEVOLVED DECISION MAKING IN SCOTLAND

Question A1

The distribution of reserved and devolved powers means that the most important decisions for Scotland continue to be made at Westminster.

Discuss.

STUDY THEME 1B: DECISION MAKING IN CENTRAL GOVERNMENT

Question A2

To what extent can Parliament control the powers of the Prime Minister?

STUDY THEME 1C: POLITICAL PARTIES AND THEIR POLICIES
(INCLUDING THE SCOTTISH DIMENSION)

Question A3

Assess the importance of party unity in achieving electoral success.

STUDY THEME 1D: ELECTORAL SYSTEMS, VOTING AND POLITICAL
ATTITUDES

Question A4

The Additional Member System gives voters more choice and better representation than does First Past The Post.

Discuss.

SECTION B — Social Issues in the United Kingdom

Each question is worth 15 marks

STUDY THEME 2: WEALTH AND HEALTH INEQUALITIES IN THE UNITED KINGDOM

EITHER

Question B5

To what extent are the founding principles of the Welfare State being met?

OR

Question B6

To what extent do social and economic inequalities continue to exist in the UK?

[Turn over

SECTION C — International Issues
Each question is worth 15 marks

STUDY THEME 3A: THE REPUBLIC OF SOUTH AFRICA

Question C7

Its political system has all the features of a democracy but South Africa has become a one party state.

Discuss.

STUDY THEME 3B: THE PEOPLE'S REPUBLIC OF CHINA

Question C8

Critically examine the effects of social and economic reform in China.

STUDY THEME 3C: THE UNITED STATES OF AMERICA

Question C9

To what extent do ethnic minorities influence the outcome of elections in the USA?

STUDY THEME 3D: THE EUROPEAN UNION

Question C10

To what extent is there agreement amongst member states on EU social and economic policies?

STUDY THEME 3E: THE POLITICS OF DEVELOPMENT IN AFRICA

Question C11

With reference to specific African countries (excluding the Republic of South Africa):

Foreign aid alone is no guarantee of development.

Discuss.

STUDY THEME 3F: GLOBAL SECURITY

Question C12

Critically examine the effectiveness of international responses to threats to global security.

[END OF QUESTION PAPER]

X236/302

NATIONAL QUALIFICATIONS 2007	TUESDAY, 22 MAY 10.50 AM – 12.50 PM	MODERN STUDIES HIGHER Paper 2

Summary of Decision Making Exercise

You are a social policy researcher. You have been asked to prepare a report for a committee investigating welfare provision in which you recommend or reject the proposal to introduce an Employment and Support Allowance (ESA).

Before beginning the task, you must answer a number of evaluating questions (Questions 1–3) based on the source material provided. The source material is:

SOURCE A: ESA will be fairer

SOURCE B: ESA will increase hardship

SOURCE C: Statistical Information

SCOTTISH QUALIFICATIONS AUTHORITY ©

SOURCE A: ESA WILL BE FAIRER

Incapacity Benefit is meant to provide an income for people who are unable to work because of medical reasons. It is the single most costly benefit that applies to people of working age.   The number of people claiming Incapacity Benefit has grown to 2·7 million. Most, but not all of these claimants, are genuinely disabled or suffering
5   from a health condition that prevents them from working. In Scotland, over 300,000 people receive Incapacity Benefit. In Glasgow, one in five of those of working age claim this benefit. Incapacity Benefit increases after six months and again after a year. It is paid for life and may be accompanied by other benefits. Incapacity Benefit discourages people from seeking work. No wonder long-term sickness and disability is the most
10   common reason given by both men and women for not working. It is not just older workers who qualify for Incapacity Benefit – each month over a thousand teenagers claim it. We are encouraging welfare dependency at the expense of individual responsibility. Incapacity Benefit needs reform.

Our proposed Employment and Support Allowance (ESA) will be fairer to new
15   claimants and give the taxpayer better value for their money. It will pay more than Incapacity Benefit but new applicants will face rigorous medical tests to prove that they are entitled to it. Those judged capable of work will have to attend "work-focused interviews" and take part in "work-related activities". At these interviews employment advisers will be available to help place people in appropriate employment. Claimants
20   who refuse to attend for interview will have their payments cut. Those who take up employment will qualify for extra benefits. The practice of increasing benefits over time will be scrapped.

The UK already spends a greater percentage of its Gross Domestic Product (GDP) on schemes for disabled workers than any other country in the European Union. We are
25   determined to continue to move people from welfare into work. Our proposed reform should lead to a million fewer Incapacity Benefit claimants by 2016. The social and economic benefits of work to the individual are obvious. New technology ensures that work is now less physically demanding. Savings made from the reform of Incapacity Benefit will, of course, be welcome. However, our main aim is to return to the
30   fundamental principles of the welfare state. It is surely far better to help people into the workplace than to condemn them to a life on benefits!

Russell Barclay, Department for Work and Pensions (DWP) Spokesperson

SOURCE B: ESA WILL INCREASE HARDSHIP

In the UK today, more people than ever are in need of support from public funds. There are 7 million people of working age with either a mental or physical disability. Charities raise millions of pounds to plug the income and health gaps in the welfare state. They already spend more on the disabled than on any other group. Yet surely it is
5   the responsibility of the state – not charities – to support people in need. There may well be 2·7 million who claim Incapacity Benefit but the number actually receiving Incapacity Benefit fell from 1·9 million in 1995 to 1·7 million in 2004, as so many claimants are turned down. This shows how tough the rules are already.

Politicians should not complain about the cost of the welfare state, and certainly never
10   about Incapacity Benefit. During the 1980s, it was government policy to encourage people to claim Incapacity Benefit in order to hide the true level of unemployment. Now, the Government will increase hardship by discouraging people from claiming a benefit to which they should be entitled. Disability experts forecast big problems in deciding who is fit enough to work. Mistakes will be made. Many claimants will be
15   unable to cope with the stress of attending interviews. Others will be pressed into taking and keeping jobs for which they are neither physically nor mentally fit. It is disgraceful that those with disabilities, and other groups vulnerable to poverty, such as lone-parents, are being forced into employment situations that they are unable to cope with. "Welfare to Work" policies are clearly more about saving money than meeting needs.

20   We live in an unequal society where there are obstacles to employment for many disabled people. Around a million people who want to work cannot find jobs, as employers are reluctant to take on staff with disabilities or other health problems. UK Government spending on the sick and disabled is already lower than for any other group and a lower percentage of one-parent families receive Incapacity/Disability Benefit than any other
25   benefit. Effective laws to prevent discrimination against the disabled would be far more useful than making the rules for Incapacity Benefit even tougher. We fully support any proposals that help disabled people to get jobs but we totally oppose this proposed reform of Incapacity Benefit. An Employment and Support Allowance (ESA) will only lead to more social exclusion and undermine the collectivist principles of the welfare
30   state.

Irene Graham, Disability Support Group (DSG) Spokesperson

[Turn over for Source C on *Pages four* and *five*

SOURCE C: STATISTICAL INFORMATION

SOURCE C1:   Reasons given by people of working age for not working

Male	Reasons	Female
%		%
37	Long-term sickness/disability	21
6	Looking after family/home	45
30	Student	19
13	Early retirement	4
14	Other	11

Source: Adapted from Labour Force Survey, Office for National Statistics

SOURCE C2:

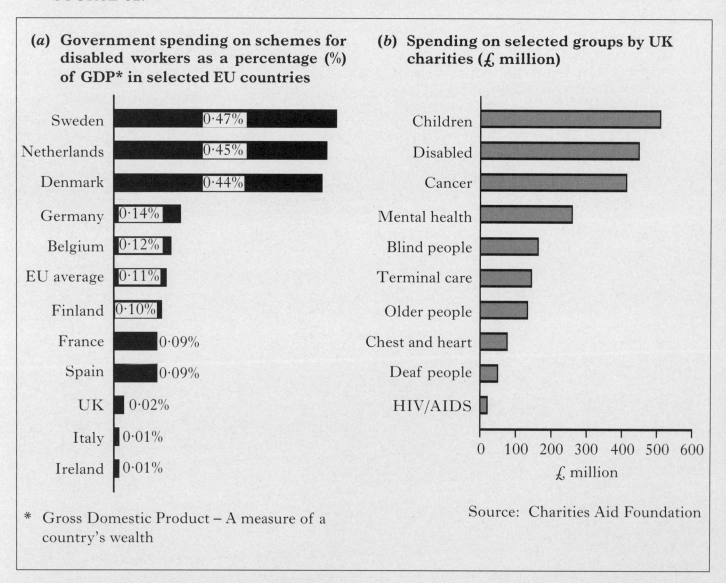

(a) Government spending on schemes for disabled workers as a percentage (%) of GDP* in selected EU countries

- Sweden 0·47%
- Netherlands 0·45%
- Denmark 0·44%
- Germany 0·14%
- Belgium 0·12%
- EU average 0·11%
- Finland 0·10%
- France 0·09%
- Spain 0·09%
- UK 0·02%
- Italy 0·01%
- Ireland 0·01%

(b) Spending on selected groups by UK charities (£ million)

- Children
- Disabled
- Cancer
- Mental health
- Blind people
- Terminal care
- Older people
- Chest and heart
- Deaf people
- HIV/AIDS

0   100   200   300   400   500   600
£ million

Source: Charities Aid Foundation

* Gross Domestic Product – A measure of a country's wealth

SOURCE C: (CONTINUED)

SOURCE C3:

(*a*) Percentage (%) share, by group, of UK Government benefit spending

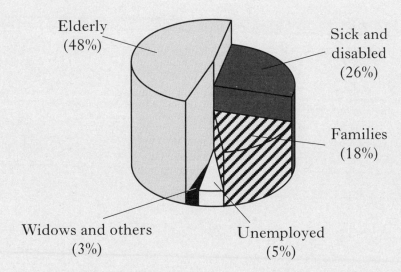

Elderly (48%)

Sick and disabled (26%)

Families (18%)

Widows and others (3%)

Unemployed (5%)

Source: Adapted from Department for Work and Pensions

(*b*) Percentage (%) of one-parent families receiving selected benefits

Benefit	(%)
Child	97
Working Families Tax Credit, Income Support **or** Minimum Income Guarantee	76
Incapacity/Disability	9
Council Tax	49
Housing	48

Source: Adapted from Family Resources Survey, Department for Work and Pensions

---

[BLANK PAGE]

DECISION MAKING EXERCISE

QUESTIONS

Marks

Questions 1 to 3 are based on Sources A to C on pages 2–5. Answer Questions 1 to 3 before attempting Question 4.

In Questions 1 to 3, use <u>only</u> the Sources described in each question.

Question 1   *Use* **only** *Source C1 and Source A.*

To what extent does the evidence support Russell Barclay?

3

Question 2

(*a*)   *Use* **only** *Source C2(a) and Source A.*

Why might Russell Barclay be accused of exaggeration?

2

(*b*)   *Use* **only** *Source C2(b) and Source B.*

Why might Irene Graham be accused of exaggeration?

2

Question 3   *Use* **only** *Source C3(a), Source C3(b) and Source B.*

To what extent does the evidence support Irene Graham?

3

(10)

Marks

Question 4

DECISION MAKING TASK

You are a social policy researcher. You have been asked to prepare a report for a committee investigating welfare provision in which you recommend or reject the proposal to introduce an Employment and Support Allowance (ESA).

Your answer should be written in a style appropriate to a *report*.

Your report should:

- recommend or reject the proposal to introduce an Employment and Support Allowance (ESA)

- provide arguments to support your decision

- identify and comment on any arguments which may be presented by those who oppose your decision

- refer to all the Sources provided

  AND

- **must** include relevant background knowledge.

The written and statistical sources which have been provided are:

SOURCE A: ESA will be fairer

SOURCE B: ESA will increase hardship

SOURCE C: Statistical Information

(20)

Total: 30 Marks

[END OF QUESTION PAPER]

[BLANK PAGE]

X236/301

NATIONAL
QUALIFICATIONS
2008

THURSDAY, 29 MAY
9.00 AM – 10.30 AM

MODERN STUDIES
HIGHER
Paper 1

Candidates should answer **FOUR** questions:

- **ONE** from Section A

and

- **ONE** from Section B

and

- **ONE** from Section C

and

- **ONE OTHER** from **EITHER** Section A **OR** Section C

Section A: Political Issues in the United Kingdom.

Section B: Social Issues in the United Kingdom.

Section C: International Issues.

Each question is worth 15 marks.

SECTION A—Political Issues in the United Kingdom
Each question is worth 15 marks

STUDY THEME 1A: DEVOLVED DECISION MAKING IN SCOTLAND

Question A1

Critically examine the role of local government in a devolved Scotland.

STUDY THEME 1B: DECISION MAKING IN CENTRAL GOVERNMENT

Question A2

Assess the effectiveness of pressure groups in influencing decision-making in Central Government.

STUDY THEME 1C: POLITICAL PARTIES AND THEIR POLICIES (INCLUDING THE SCOTTISH DIMENSION)

Question A3

There are few policy differences between the main political parties.
Discuss.

STUDY THEME 1D: ELECTORAL SYSTEMS, VOTING AND POLITICAL ATTITUDES

Question A4

Assess the influence of social class on voting behaviour.

SECTION B — Social Issues in the United Kingdom

Each question is worth 15 marks

STUDY THEME 2: WEALTH AND HEALTH INEQUALITIES IN THE UNITED KINGDOM

EITHER

Question B5

Assess the effectiveness of government policies to reduce gender and ethnic inequalities.

OR

Question B6

Critically examine the view that government, not individuals, should be responsible for health care and welfare provision.

[Turn over

SECTION C — International Issues
Each question is worth 15 marks

STUDY THEME 3A: THE REPUBLIC OF SOUTH AFRICA

Question C7

Assess the effectiveness of Black Economic Empowerment in reducing inequalities.

STUDY THEME 3B: THE PEOPLE'S REPUBLIC OF CHINA

Question C8

Critically examine the view that China is becoming a more democratic society.

STUDY THEME 3C: THE UNITED STATES OF AMERICA

Question C9

Assess the effectiveness of Congress and the Supreme Court in checking the powers of the President.

STUDY THEME 3D: THE EUROPEAN UNION

Question C10

Assess the impact of enlargement on the European Union.

STUDY THEME 3E: THE POLITICS OF DEVELOPMENT IN AFRICA

Question C11

With reference to specific African countries (excluding the Republic of South Africa):

Assess the importance of education and health care to successful development.

STUDY THEME 3F: GLOBAL SECURITY

Question C12

Critically examine the part played by the USA in achieving global security.

[END OF QUESTION PAPER]

X236/302

NATIONAL QUALIFICATIONS 2008	THURSDAY, 29 MAY 10.50 AM – 12.05 PM	MODERN STUDIES HIGHER Paper 2

Summary of Decision Making Exercise

You are an expert on social policy. You have been asked to prepare a report for an all-party group of MSPs, in which you recommend or reject the proposal to make all prescriptions free in Scotland.

Before beginning the task, you must answer a number of evaluating questions (Questions 1–3) based on the source material provided. The source material is:

SOURCE A: Prescription Charges are a Danger to Health

SOURCE B: Prescription Charges are Necessary

SOURCE C: Statistical Information

SOURCE A: PRESCRIPTION CHARGES ARE A DANGER TO HEALTH

The Scottish Government is to be commended for its determination to phase out and eventually abolish prescription charges. Since first introduced, prescription charges have been kept ever since, except for a brief period of abolition in the 1960s. Although large numbers of prescriptions are dispensed free, the price per item is such that many
5   adults find it very difficult to pay.

Since April 2007, all patients registered with a Welsh GP, who get their prescriptions from a Welsh pharmacist, have been entitled to free prescriptions. There is no evidence that this has led to an increased demand for prescriptions in Wales. The suggestion that people ask for unnecessary prescriptions is ridiculous. The most common reasons for
10   not handing in a prescription are to do with cost—no one finds that they did not need it after all. Prescription charges prevent the sick from getting essential medicines. Being forced to decide which item on a prescription they can afford is one choice that patients can do without. The effects of this on individuals, and in the longer term on the National Health Service (NHS), should be obvious! Interrupting or delaying treatment
15   for just a few days can increase the risks to one's health. The long-term costs to the NHS become much greater because hospital treatment that could have been avoided becomes necessary.   GPs have become so concerned about the consequences of prescription charges that one in five has admitted to falsifying paperwork to ensure that vulnerable patients get free prescriptions.

20   The prescription charge is a tax on the sick and not at all in keeping with the founding principles of the NHS. Furthermore, it undermines any attempts to tackle the health divide in a society in which the link between deprivation and ill health has been clearly established. The pre-payment certificate only benefits those who can afford it. There is no way that patients on low incomes can afford to pay the required lump sum in
25   advance. The actual revenue gained from prescription charges is a tiny proportion of the estimated £10 billion budget for the NHS in Scotland. Making all prescriptions free in Scotland would be straightforward, effective and fair. Free prescriptions would make a huge difference as to whether people would or would not go to a doctor. There would be an immediate improvement in the health of the nation from which future generations
30   would only benefit.

Daphne Millar, Anti-Poverty Campaigner

SOURCE B: PRESCRIPTION CHARGES ARE NECESSARY

Within a few years of the creation of the NHS, a charge for each item on a prescription was introduced in response to the rising costs of medicines. However, children under 16 and men and women aged 60 and over get free prescriptions. Other categories of people are also entitled to exemption from NHS prescription charges. Around half of the
5 population qualify for free prescriptions. This results in 90% of dispensed prescription items being issued free of charge. For those who do have to pay, there is a system of pre-payment certificates. This gives unlimited prescriptions for up to twelve months for a one-off payment. Furthermore, almost two ·in every three medicines available on prescription can be bought more cheaply over the counter. Despite prescription charges,
10 the NHS has always enjoyed strong public support. In a recent survey on health care systems in European countries, the UK was one of the highest rated.

The UK Government intends to keep prescription charges in England. The Scottish Government must keep them too. It is estimated that in the financial year 2007–2008, prescription charges brought in a much-needed £46 million in revenue to the NHS in
15 Scotland. Such a sum buys a lot of health care, be it equipment or staff. Abolish charges, and the demand for unnecessary prescriptions will surely increase. GPs are concerned about the number of patients who consult them for no good medical reason. If charges are abolished, the number of patients asking doctors for unnecessary prescriptions will increase. This will put pressure on the drugs budget and may mean
20 delays in introducing life saving but expensive new drugs.

Abolishing prescription charges will not help those on low incomes. It will divert resources towards those on middle and upper incomes. Most people who have to pay can afford all of the items on their prescriptions and there is little support from health and community groups for completely abolishing prescription charges. Abolishing
25 prescription charges would have a bad effect on both the financing and performance of the NHS in Scotland. The resulting cutbacks in the provision of care would hit the poorest members of society the most. Prescription charges must be retained if the health gap is to be closed.

Tom Beattie, Health Economist

[Turn over for Source C on *Pages four* and *five*

SOURCE C: STATISTICAL INFORMATION

SOURCE C1: Public opinion survey results

(*a*) **Reasons patients gave for not handing in prescriptions**

It cost less to buy the medicine over the counter	28%
It cost too much money (£6·85 per item)	25%
Health improved – did not need it after all	10%
I wanted to wait and see if I felt better	16%
I didn't feel I was prescribed the correct medicine	11%
I had some medicine left from the last time	5%
I forgot about it	5%

Source: Adapted from Consultation on Review of NHS Prescription Charges
(Scotland) 2007

(*b*) **If all prescriptions became free, in what way would it influence your decision to go to the doctor?**

% of people surveyed

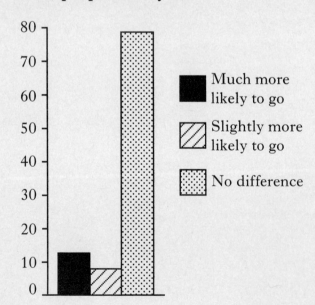

- ■ Much more likely to go
- ▨ Slightly more likely to go
- ▦ No difference

Source: Adapted from Consultation on Review of NHS Prescription Charges (Scotland) 2007

(*c*) **In the past year, how many items on your prescriptions have you been able to afford?**

% of people surveyed

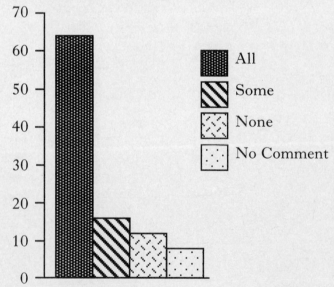

- ■ All
- ▨ Some
- ▦ None
- ⠿ No Comment

Source: Adapted from National Association of Citizens Advice Bureaux data 2001

SOURCE C: **(CONTINUED)**

SOURCE C2:   **How people rate their health care systems (perfect score 100)**

Country	Score
Belgium	66
France	65
Germany	76
Hungary	58
Italy	48
Netherlands	80
Poland	41
Spain	61
Sweden	66
Switzerland	78
UK	60

Source: Adapted from *The Times*, June 2005

SOURCE C3:   **Results of consultation with health and community groups**

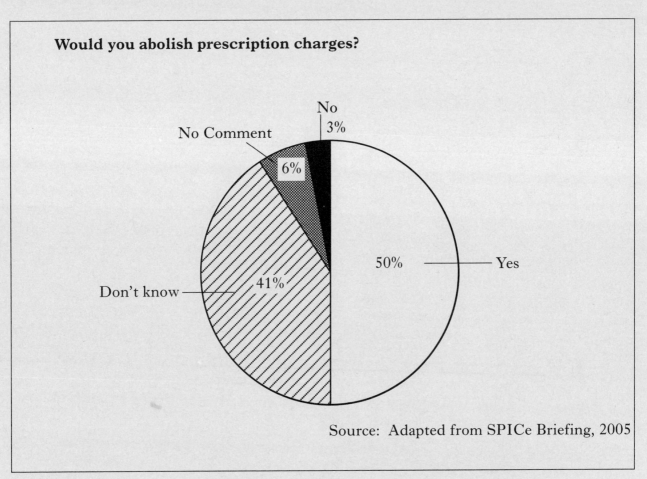

Source: Adapted from SPICe Briefing, 2005

[BLANK PAGE]

DECISION MAKING EXERCISE

QUESTIONS

Marks

Questions 1 to 3 are based on Sources A to C on pages 2–5. Answer Questions 1 to 3 before attempting Question 4.

In Questions 1 to 3, use <u>only</u> the Sources described in each question.

Question 1　*Use* **only** *Source C1(a) and Source A.*

To what extent does the evidence support Daphne Millar?　　　　　　**3**

Question 2

(*a*)　*Use* **only** *Source C1(b) and Source A.*

　　Why might Daphne Millar be accused of exaggeration?　　　　　**2**

(*b*)　*Use* **only** *Source C2 and Source B.*

　　Why might Tom Beattie be accused of exaggeration?　　　　　　**2**

Question 3　*Use* **only** *Source C1(c) and Source C3 and Source B.*

To what extent does the evidence support Tom Beattie?　　　　　　**3**

(10)

Marks

Question 4

DECISION MAKING TASK

You are an expert on social policy. You have been asked to prepare a report for an all-party group of MSPs, in which you recommend or reject the proposal to make all prescriptions free in Scotland.

Your answer should be written in a style of a *report*.

Your report should:

- recommend or reject the proposal to make all prescriptions free in Scotland

- provide arguments to support your decision

- identify and comment on any arguments which may be presented by those who oppose your decision

- refer to all the Sources provided

  AND

- **must** include relevant background knowledge.

The written and statistical sources which have been provided are:

SOURCE A: Prescription Charges are a Danger to Health

SOURCE B: Prescription Charges are Necessary

SOURCE C: Statistical Information

(20)

Total: 30 Marks

[END OF QUESTION PAPER]

[BLANK PAGE]

X236/301

NATIONAL
QUALIFICATIONS
2009

MONDAY, 25 MAY
9.00 AM – 10.30 AM

MODERN STUDIES
HIGHER
Paper 1

Candidates should answer **FOUR** questions:

- **ONE** from Section A

and

- **ONE** from Section B

and

- **ONE** from Section C

and

- **ONE OTHER** from **EITHER** Section A **OR** Section C

Section A: Political Issues in the United Kingdom.

Section B: Social Issues in the United Kingdom.

Section C: International Issues.

Each question is worth 15 marks.

SECTION A—Political Issues in the United Kingdom
Each question is worth 15 marks

STUDY THEME 1A: DEVOLVED DECISION MAKING IN SCOTLAND

Question A1

Assess the impact of devolution on decision making for Scotland.

STUDY THEME 1B: DECISION MAKING IN CENTRAL GOVERNMENT

Question A2

Backbench MPs have little influence on decision making in Central Government.

Discuss.

*STUDY THEME 1C: POLITICAL PARTIES AND THEIR POLICIES
(INCLUDING THE SCOTTISH DIMENSION)*

Question A3

To what extent are there ideological differences within and between the main political parties?

*STUDY THEME 1D: ELECTORAL SYSTEMS, VOTING AND POLITICAL
ATTITUDES*

Question A4

Critically examine the view that the media is the most important influence on voting behaviour.

SECTION B — Social Issues in the United Kingdom

Each question is worth 15 marks

STUDY THEME 2: WEALTH AND HEALTH INEQUALITIES IN THE UNITED KINGDOM

EITHER

Question B5

Assess the impact of income on health.

OR

Question B6

Critically examine the success of recent government policies to reduce poverty.

[Turn over for Section C on *Page four*

SECTION C — International Issues

Each question is worth 15 marks

STUDY THEME 3A: THE REPUBLIC OF SOUTH AFRICA

Question C7

Critically examine the view that inequalities exist only *between* different racial groups.

STUDY THEME 3B: THE PEOPLE'S REPUBLIC OF CHINA

Question C8

Critically examine the view that there is little demand for political reform because of greater social and economic freedom.

STUDY THEME 3C: THE UNITED STATES OF AMERICA

Question C9

To what extent do ethnic minorities achieve the American Dream?

STUDY THEME 3D: THE EUROPEAN UNION

Question C10

The Council of Ministers is the most important decision-making institution in the EU.

Discuss.

STUDY THEME 3E: THE POLITICS OF DEVELOPMENT IN AFRICA

Question C11

With reference to specific African countries (excluding the Republic of South Africa):

Assess the influence of Non Governmental Organisations on development.

STUDY THEME 3F: GLOBAL SECURITY

Question C12

Assess the effectiveness of the United Nations in dealing with threats to international peace and security.

[END OF QUESTION PAPER]

X236/302

NATIONAL
QUALIFICATIONS
2009

MONDAY, 25 MAY
10.50 AM – 12.05 PM

MODERN STUDIES
HIGHER
Paper 2

Summary of Decision Making Exercise

You are a policy researcher in the Department for Work and Pensions. You have been asked to prepare a report in which you recommend or reject Fifty-Fifty, a proposal that women hold the same number of senior management posts in the public services as men.

Before beginning the task, you must answer a number of evaluating questions (Questions 1–3) based on the source material provided. The source material is:

SOURCE A: Fifty-Fifty will deliver equality

SOURCE B: Fifty-Fifty is not the solution

SOURCE C: Statistical Information

SOURCE A: FIFTY-FIFTY WILL DELIVER EQUALITY

The glass ceiling in the UK has proved to be very robust. Many women who choose a career path in the public services are being prevented from reaching their full potential both personally and economically. This is a waste of their talents, the money spent on their training, and a severe loss to the UK economy as a whole.

5 Fifty-Fifty will make it compulsory for women to hold the same number of senior management posts in the public services as men. Public services will be required to set out strategies on how they will meet this target. The percentage of women in senior positions in the public services is well below that of men, so it comes as no surprise that the UK has the largest gender pay gap in the European Union. The fact that in 2007
10 male staff at St Andrews University earned, on average, 23% more than their female colleagues is only one of the many examples of unequal pay to be found in the UK.

Government has a responsibility to promote equal opportunities. Yet despite over thirty years of legislation, the UK still does not have gender equality. All too often the approach of government has been to recognise that things are unfair, acknowledge that
15 "something" should be done, then ignore any advice it receives. The Women and Work Commission (2004–2006) made forty recommendations. One of these was that girls be encouraged to consider work other than catering, clerical and the rest of the "Five Cs". Even now, there is concern that many schools still stereotype girls when it comes to work experience and careers guidance.

20 Surely no one can dispute the reasons why Fifty-Fifty is necessary. We have no shortage of talented female staff in our public services. Filling posts will not be a problem. Fifty-Fifty will mean that women will be guaranteed their fair share of senior appointments. This will end gender segregation in, and bring fresh approaches to, the delivery of public services. Well over half of women say that having children is the biggest obstacle
25 they face in pursuing a successful career. For many women, motherhood effectively ends their chance of promotion. The gap between male and female opportunities and rewards is unacceptable and the current pace of progress towards equality does little for the UK's equal opportunities record. Fifty-Fifty is a practical and effective solution to a centuries old problem: the glass ceiling will be smashed once and for all.

Avril Beattie, Equal Opportunities Spokesperson

SOURCE B: FIFTY-FIFTY IS NOT THE SOLUTION

Fifty-Fifty is not the solution to gender inequalities in employment. Gender is irrelevant to a person's ability to do the job. We must never depart from the principle that senior management posts should go to the best person for the job. In any case, change is already taking place. More girls than boys are going into both full time
5   higher/further education and employment. It is only a matter of time before these high achieving girls go on to occupy top managerial posts at the expense of males.

Government has already recognised that words alone are not enough and that action must be taken to address gender inequalities. There has been a great deal of gender equality legislation in recent years. In addition, diversity targets have been set for the
10   Civil Service. We have reached a point where equality laws are actually holding back women's careers.

It should not be up to government to decide who makes it to the top posts in management. Surely it is a matter of individual choice and responsibility. There are plenty of high profile women who have achieved great success in a wide range of careers.
15   The Fifty-Fifty proposal is an insult to these high achievers. It is patronising to female staff to say that they are not good enough to get promotion on their own merits. Fifty-Fifty will only increase the time already being spent on tracking and monitoring. It will become more difficult to both recruit and retain high quality male staff. Many talented men will leave for better opportunities in the private sector. What our public services
20   need are more resources to tackle the UK's many social problems. Tackling these should be the priority for the public services, not the expense of chasing politically correct gender targets.

The UK has an excellent equal opportunities record with one of the highest percentages of women in senior management in the world. In any case, not all women want to reach
25   the dizzy heights of senior management – and the added pressure it brings. Many women have recognised the importance of a healthy work-life balance and made an informed decision to choose family life before a career. The overall gap in weekly earnings between male and female workers is tiny. Fifty-Fifty will only improve opportunities for those at the top and is by no means the solution to wider inequalities in
30   society.

Jim Waugh, Businessman

[Turn over for Source C on *Pages four* and *five*

SOURCE C: STATISTICAL INFORMATION

SOURCE C1 (*a*) Women in public service senior management in the UK, 2005 (%)

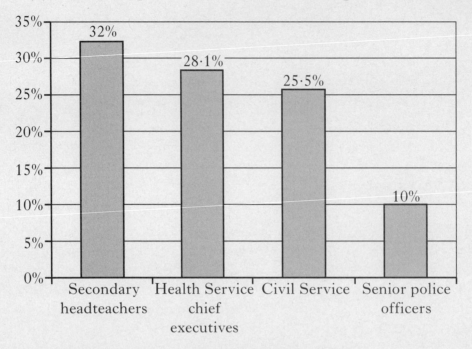

SOURCE C1 (*b*) Gender pay gap in the EU, 2005 (%)

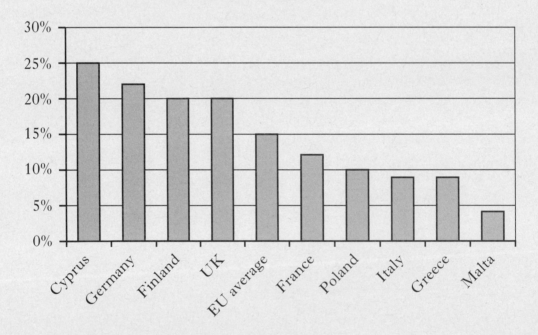

SOURCE C2 (*a*) Female public opinion survey

What is the biggest obstacle you face in pursuing a successful career?

Bad/inconsiderate attitudes in the workplace	44%
Having children	48%
Nothing: women have equal opportunities	8%

SOURCE C: (CONTINUED)

SOURCE C2 (*b*) Percentage of school leavers from state schools in Scotland by destination and gender, 2006–2007

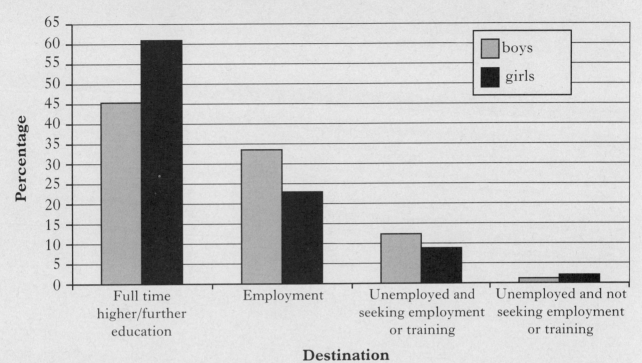

SOURCE C3 Senior management posts occupied by women in selected countries, 2006 (%)

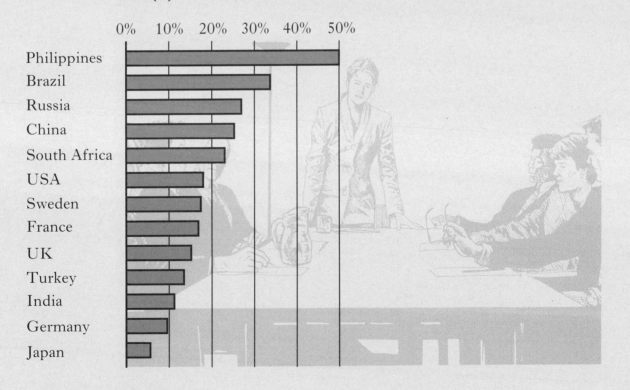

[BLANK PAGE]

DECISION MAKING EXERCISE

QUESTIONS

Marks

Questions 1 to 3 are based on Sources A to C on pages 2–5. **Answer Questions 1 to 3 before attempting Question 4.**

In Questions 1 to 3, use <u>only</u> the Sources described in each question.

Question 1   *Use* **only** *Source C1(a), Source C1(b) and Source A.*

To what extent does the evidence support the view of Avril Beattie?   **3**

Question 2

(*a*)   *Use* **only** *Source C2(a) and Source A.*

     Why might Avril Beattie be accused of exaggeration?   **2**

(*b*)   *Use* **only** *Source C2(b) and Source B.*

     To what extent does the evidence support the view of Jim Waugh?   **3**

Question 3   *Use* **only** *Source C3 and Source B.*

Why might Jim Waugh be accused of exaggeration?   **2**

         (10)

Question 4

DECISION MAKING TASK

You are a policy researcher in the Department for Work and Pensions. You have been asked to prepare a report in which you recommend or reject Fifty-Fifty, a proposal that women hold the same number of senior management posts in the public services as men.

Your answer should be written in the style of a *report*.

Your report should:

- recommend or reject Fifty-Fifty

- provide arguments to support your decision

- identify and comment on any arguments which may be presented by those who oppose your decision

- refer to all the Sources provided

  AND

- **must** include relevant background knowledge.

The written and statistical sources which are provided are:

SOURCE A: Fifty-Fifty will deliver equality

SOURCE B: Fifty-Fifty is not the solution

SOURCE C: Statistical Information

(20)

Total: 30 Marks

[END OF QUESTION PAPER]

[BLANK PAGE]

[BLANK PAGE]

[BLANK PAGE]